EASY PIANO

Produced by
Alfred Music Publishing Co., Inc.
P.O. Box 10003
Van Nuys, CA 91410-0003
alfred.com

Printed in USA.

ISBN-10: 0-7390-6704-4
ISBN-13: 978-0-7390-6704-8

CONTENTS

JAM

Lyrics by Michael Jackson
Music by Michael Jackson, Rene Moore,
Bruce Swedien and Teddy Riley
Arranged by Dan Coates

Steady funk beat
Verse:

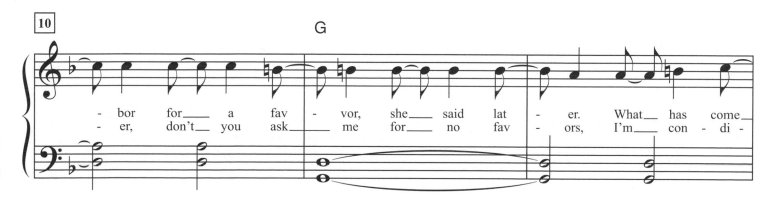

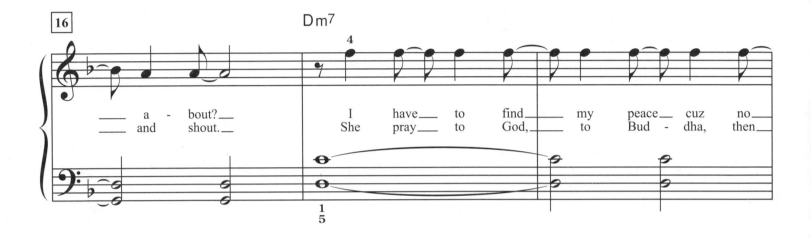

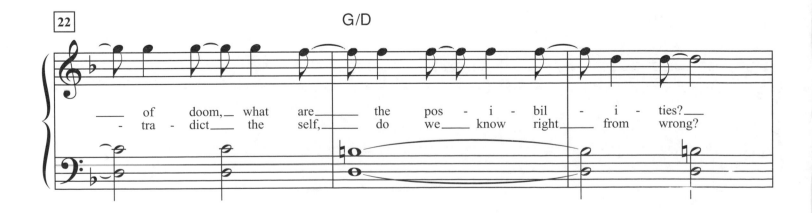

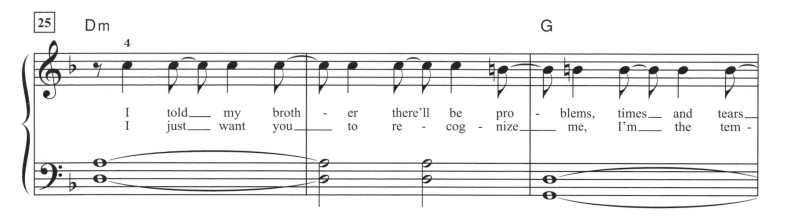

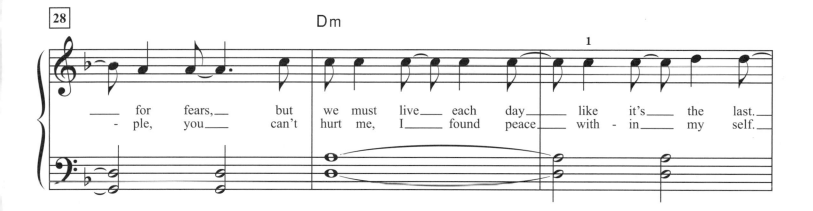

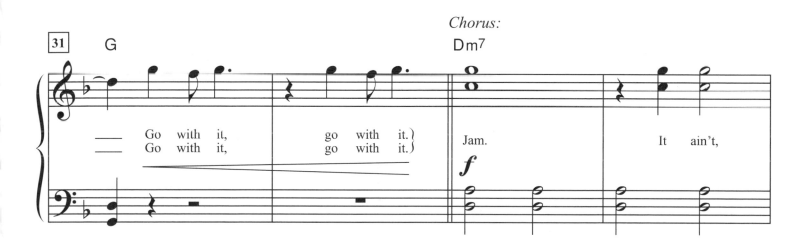

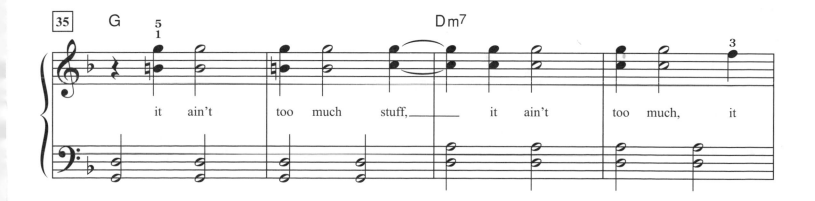

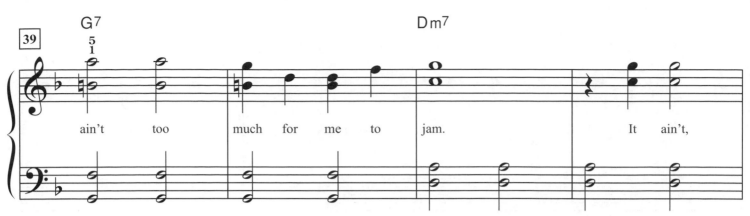

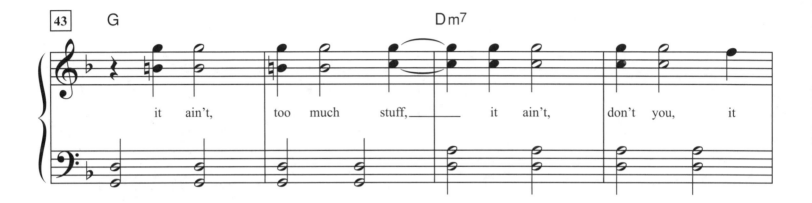

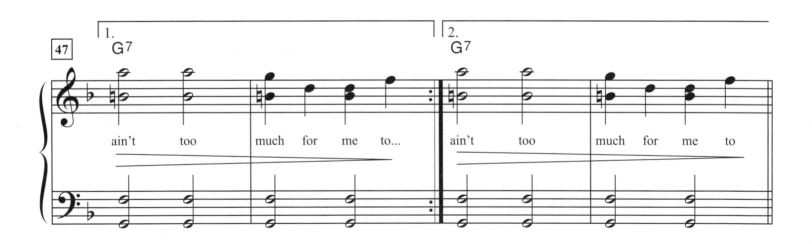

Jam. It ain't, it ain't too much stuff,___

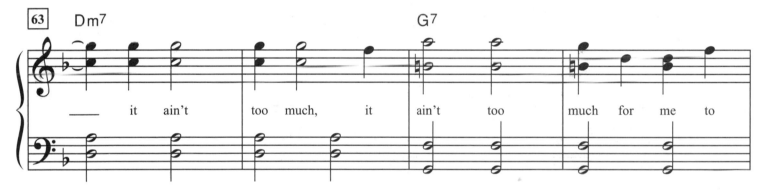

___ it ain't too much, it ain't too much for me to

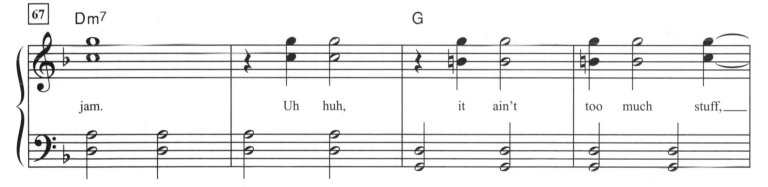

jam. Uh huh, it ain't too much stuff,___

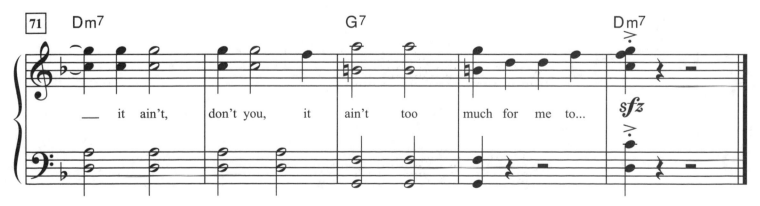

___ it ain't, don't you, it ain't too much for me to...

WANNA BE STARTIN' SOMETHIN'

Music by Michael Jackson
Arranged by Dan Coates

stuck in the mid - dle (yeah, yeah), and the pain is thun - der (yeah, yeah). It's too

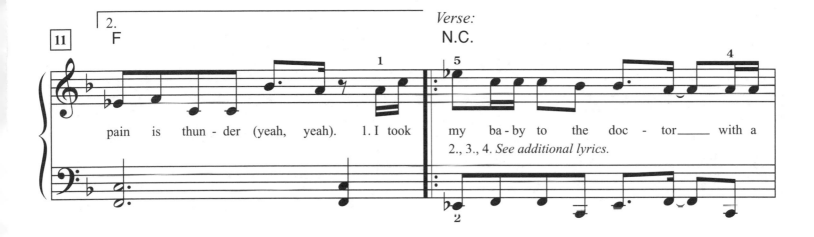

Verse:

pain is thun - der (yeah, yeah). 1. I took my ba - by to the doc - tor____ with a
2., 3., 4. *See additional lyrics.*

fe - ver, but noth - ing he found. By the time this hit the street,_____ they

said she had a break - down. Some - one's al - ways try - in' to

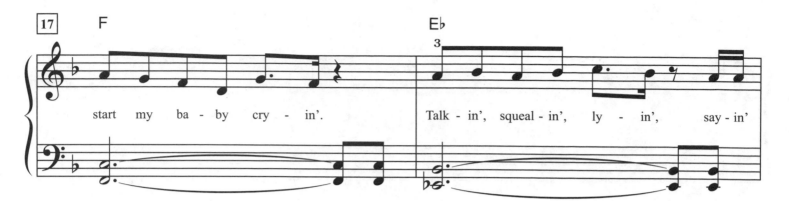

low to get un - der (Yeah, yeah). You're stuck in the mid - dle (yeah, yeah), and the

1.
pain is thun - der (yeah, yeah). 2. You

2., 3.
pain is thun - der (yeah, yeah). You're a

veg' - ta - ble, you're a veg' - ta - ble.___ Still they hate you. You're a

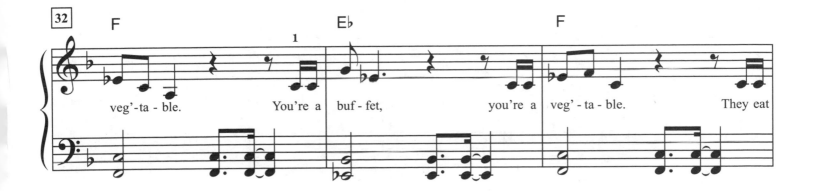

veg' - ta - ble. You're a buf - fet, you're a veg' - ta - ble. They eat

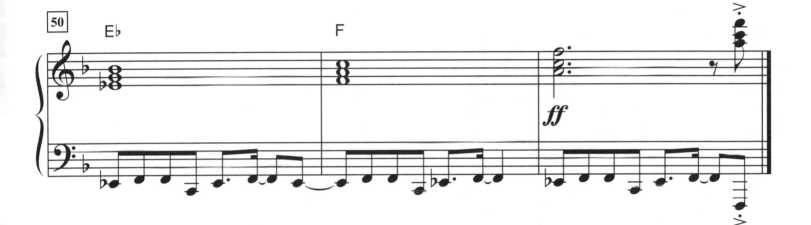

Verse 2:
You love to pretend that you're good when you're always up to no good.
You really can't make him hate her, so your tongue became a razor.
Someone's always tryin' to keep my baby cryin'.
Treacherous, cunnin', declinin'.
You got my baby cryin'.
(To Chorus:)

Verse 3:
Billie Jean is always talkin' when nobody else is talkin',
Tellin' lies and rubbin' shoulders, so they call her mouth a motor.
Someone's always tryin' to start my baby cryin'.
Talkin', squealin', spyin', sayin'
You just wanna be startin' somethin'.
(To Chorus:)

Verse 4:
If you can't feed your baby, then don't have a baby.
And don't think maybe, if you can't feed your baby.
You'll be always tryin' to stop that child from cryin'.
Hustlin', stealin', lyin'.
Now baby's slowly dyin'.
(To Chorus:)

THEY DON'T CARE ABOUT US

Written and Composed by
Michael Jackson
Arranged by Dan Coates

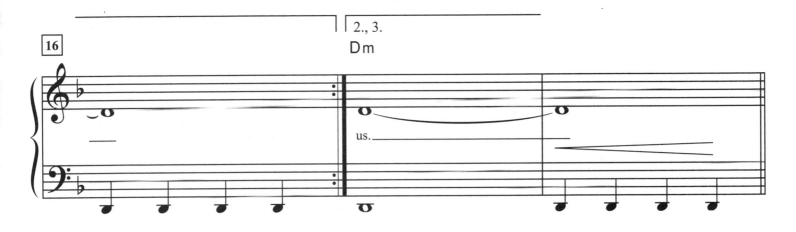

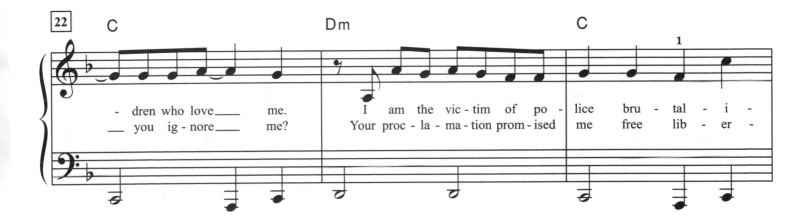

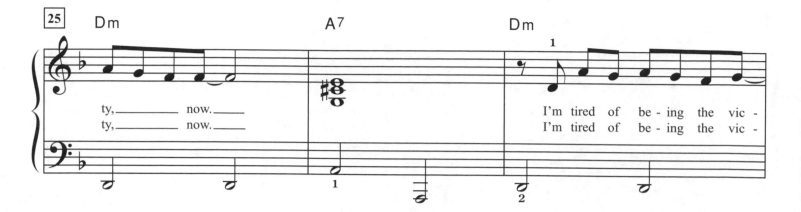

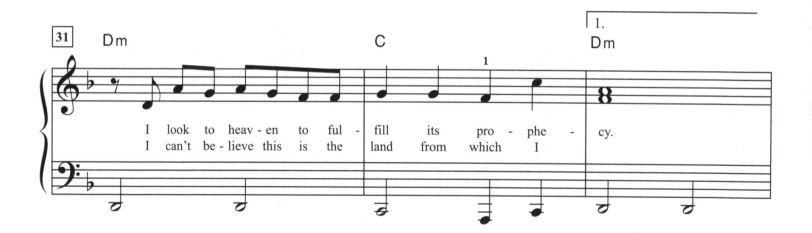

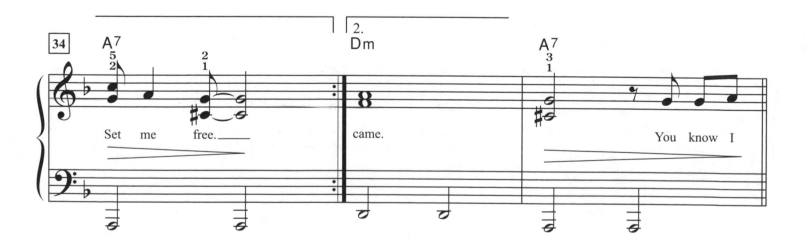

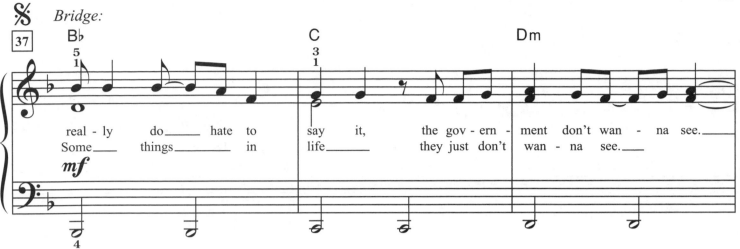

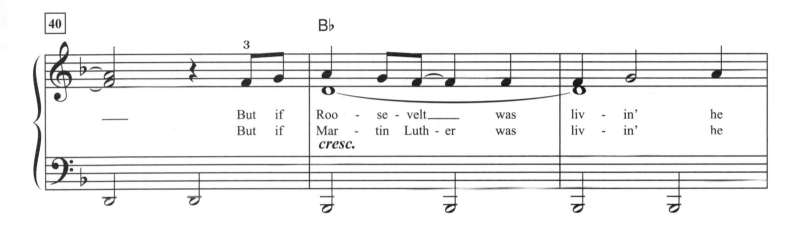

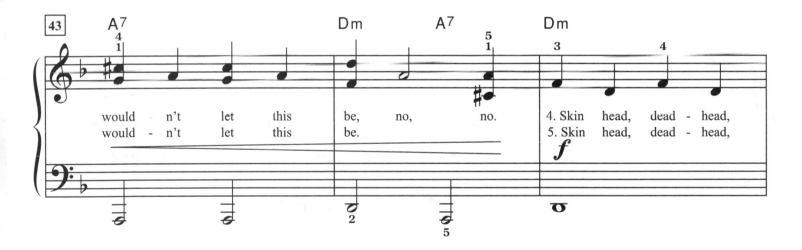

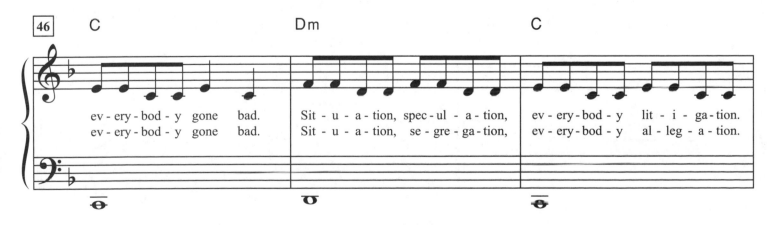

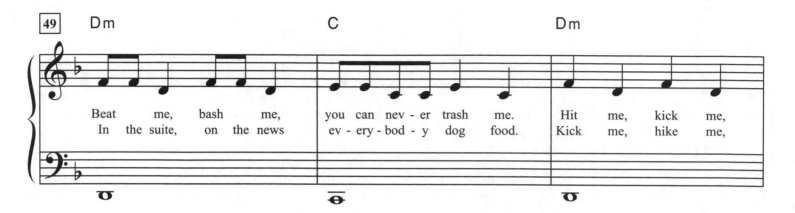

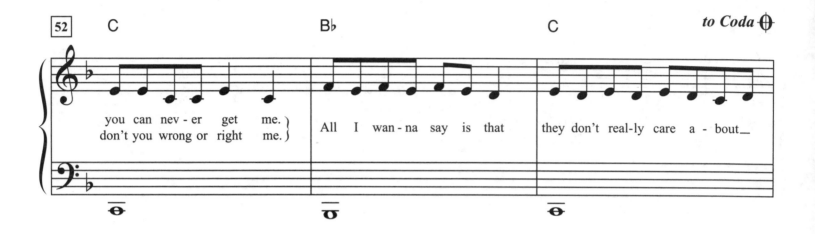

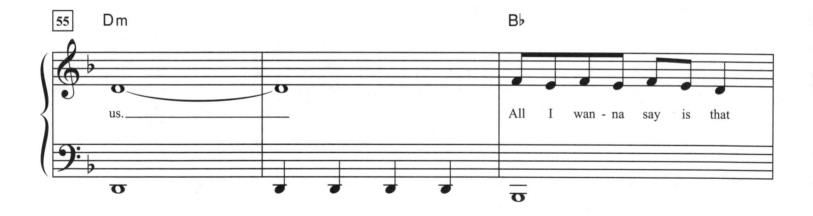

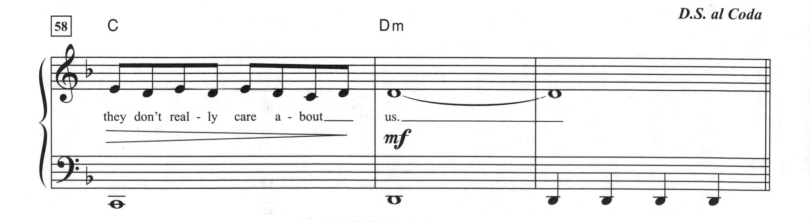

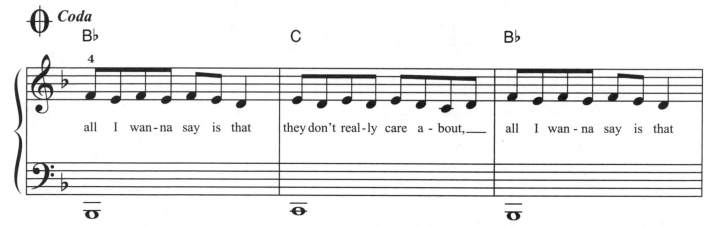

all I wan-na say is that / they don't real-ly care a-bout,___ / all I wan-na say is that

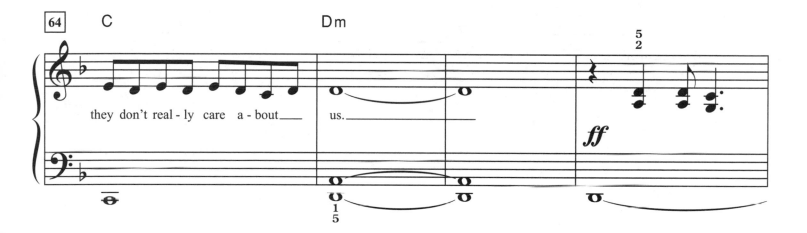

they don't real-ly care a-bout___ us.___

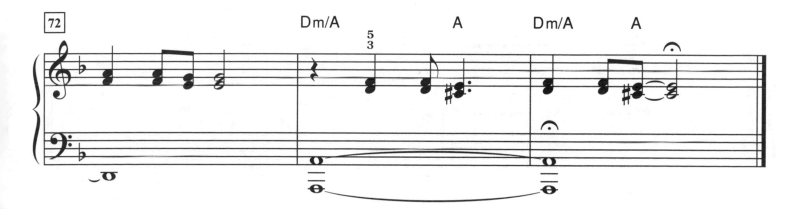

HUMAN NATURE

Words and Music by
John Bettis and Steve Porcaro
Arranged by Dan Coates

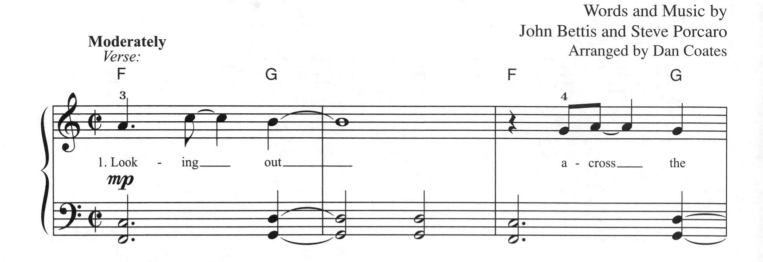

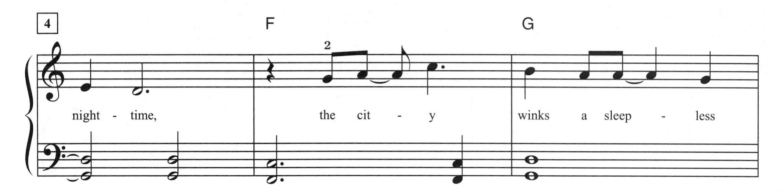

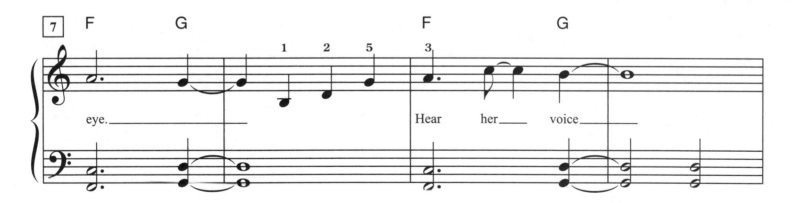

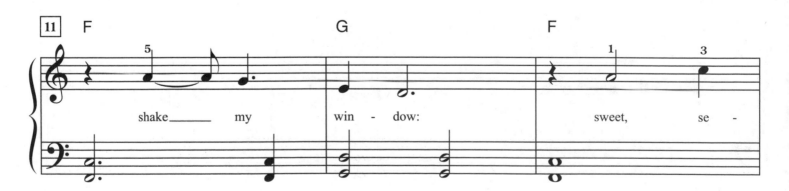

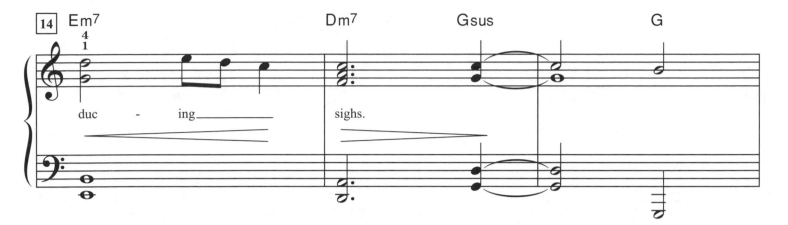

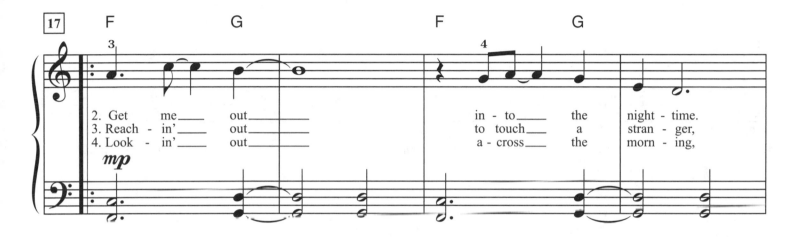

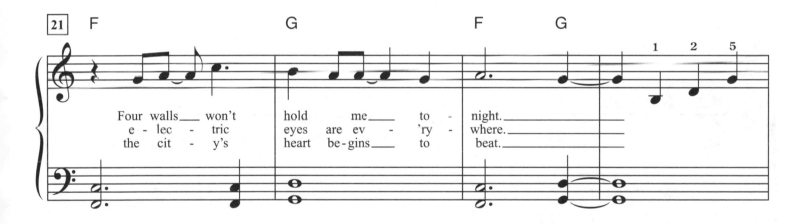

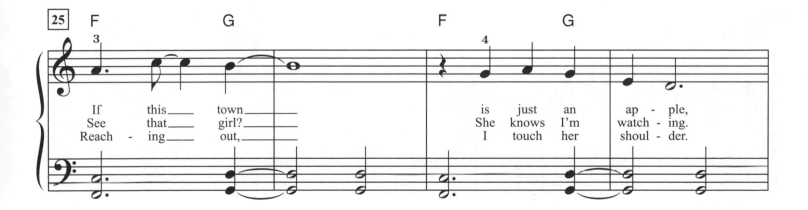

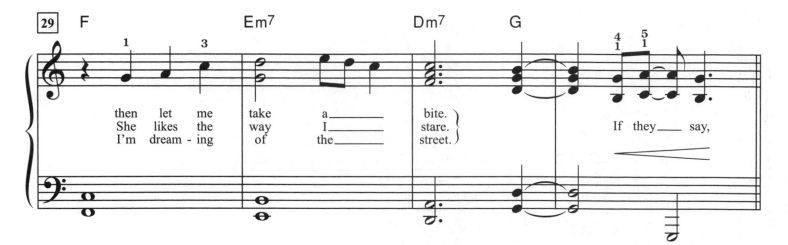

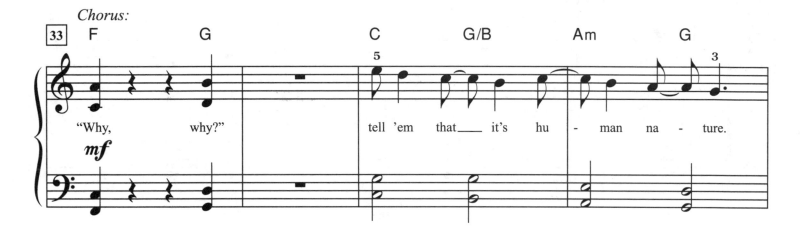

Chorus:

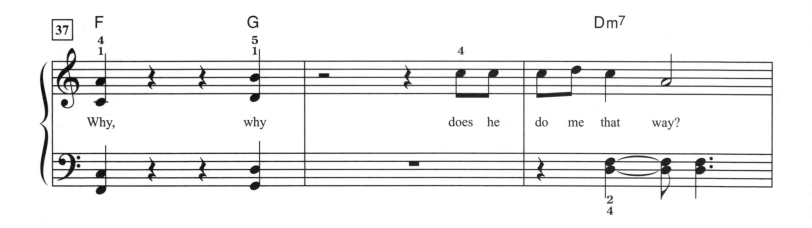

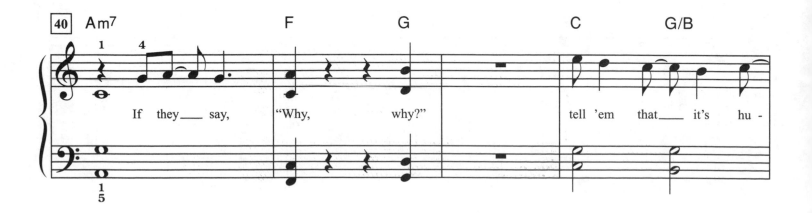

29

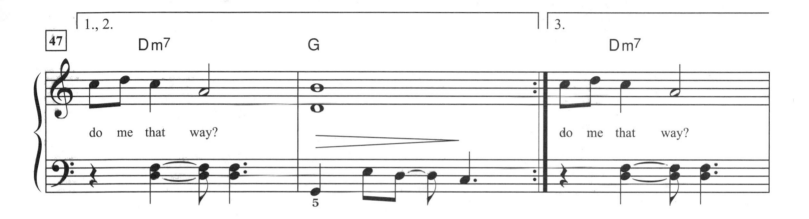

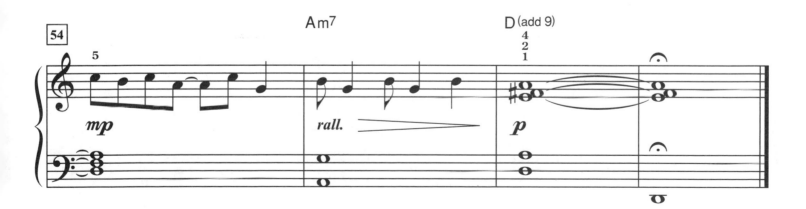

SMOOTH CRIMINAL

Written and Composed by
Michael Jackson
Arranged by Dan Coates

Moderately, with a steady beat

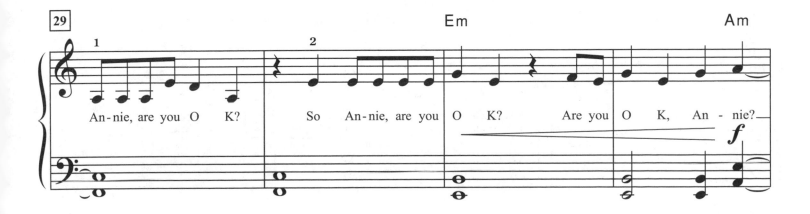

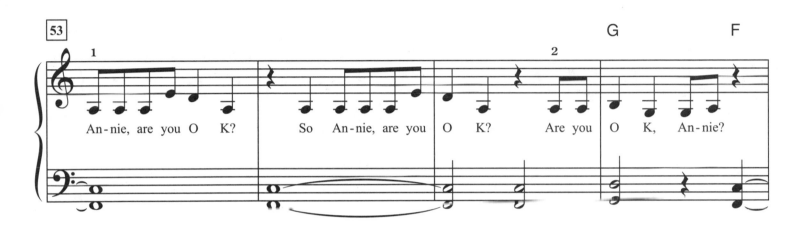

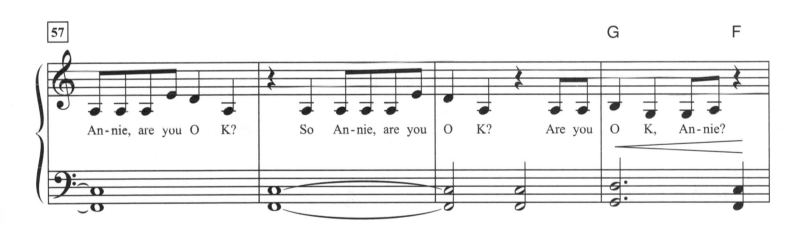

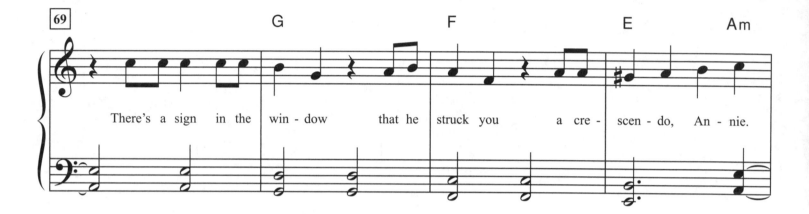

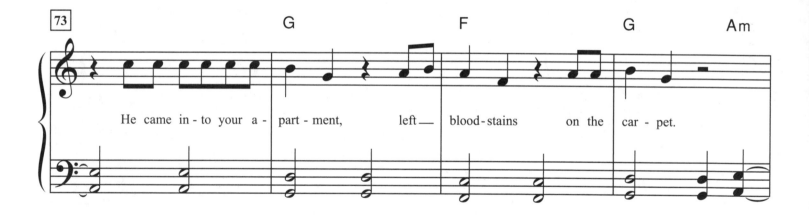

SHAKE YOUR BODY
(DOWN TO THE GROUND)

Words and Music by
Michael Joe Jackson and Randy Jackson
Arranged by Dan Coates

Moderately fast dance beat

Verse:

1. I don't know___ what's gon-na hap-pen to you,___ ba — by, but I
tease me with___ your lov-in' to play hard to___ get___ 'cause you
3., 4. *See additional lyrics.*

do know that I love ya.___ 1., 2. You
do know that I want ya.___ 3. I

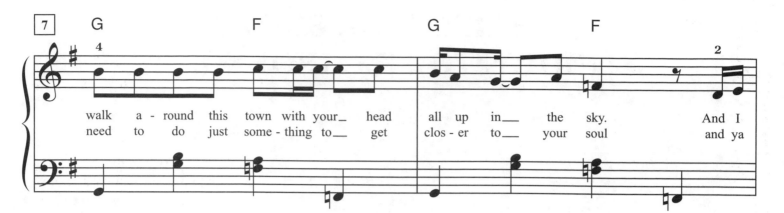

Chorus:

dance,   let's shout,   shake your bod - y down   to   the ground.____ Let's

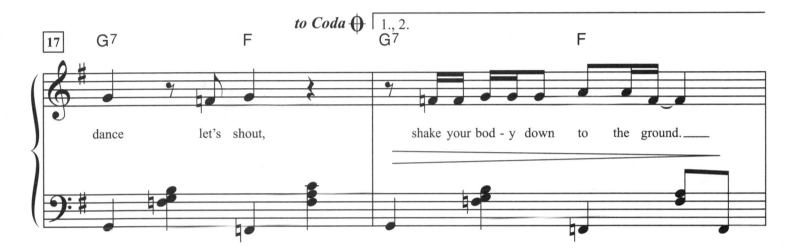

to Coda   ⊕ | 1., 2.

dance   let's shout,   shake your bod - y down   to   the ground.____

mf

2. You
3. You're

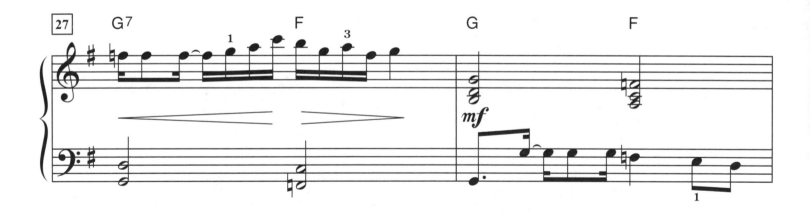

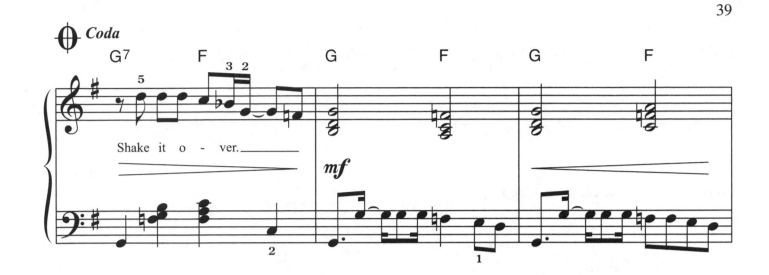

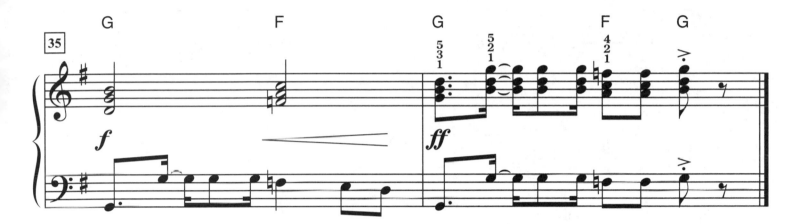

Verse 3:
You're the fire that lit the spark inside of me
And you do know that I love it.
I need to do just something to get closer to your soul
And ya do know that I want ya.
(To Chorus:)

Verse 4:
You tease me with your lovin' to play hard to get
'Cause you do know that I want ya.
I need to do just something to get closer to your soul
And you do know that I want ya.
(To Chorus:)

THE WAY YOU MAKE ME FEEL

Written and Composed by
Michael Jackson
Arranged by Dan Coates

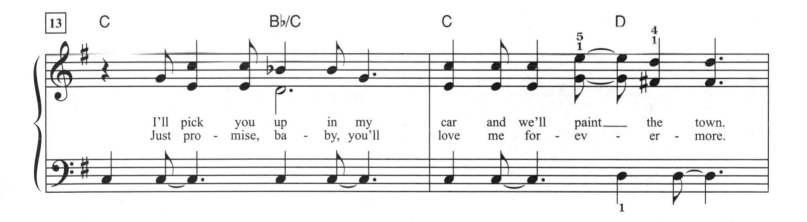

Chorus:

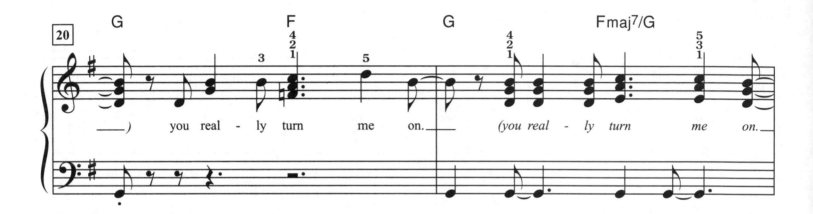

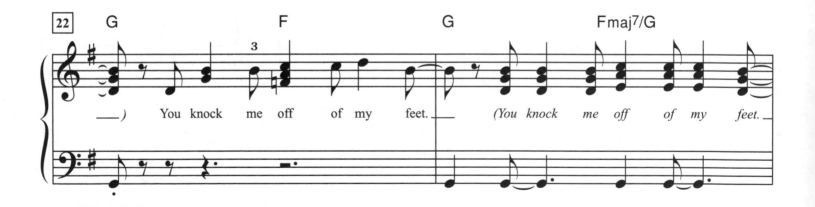

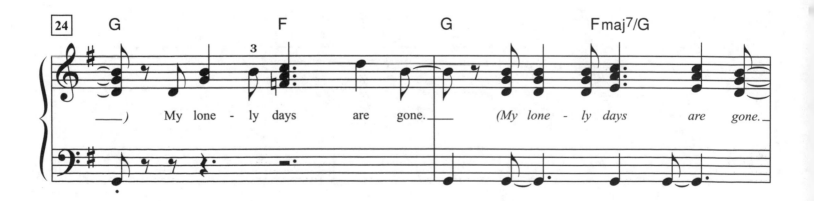

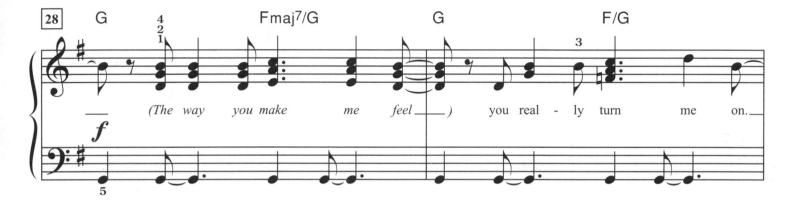

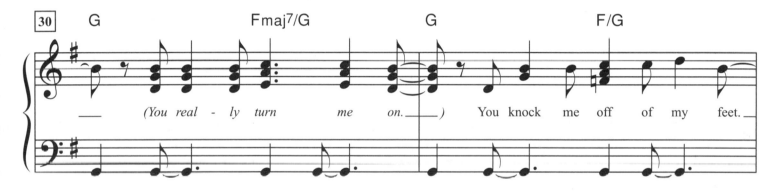

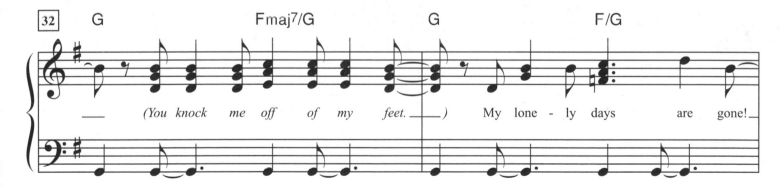

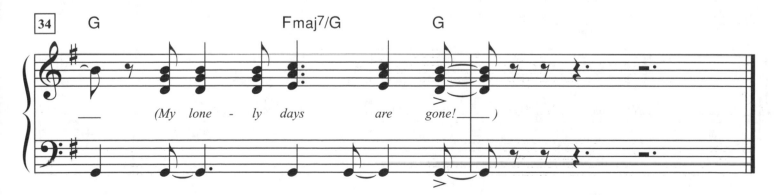

I JUST CAN'T STOP LOVING YOU

Written and Composed By
Michael Jackson
Arranged by Dan Coates

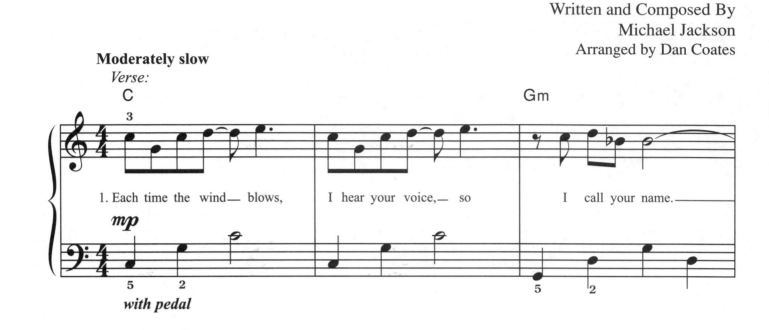

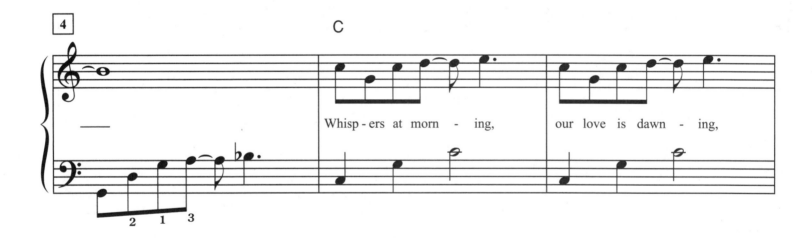

thing can't go wrong. I'm so proud to say I love you. Your

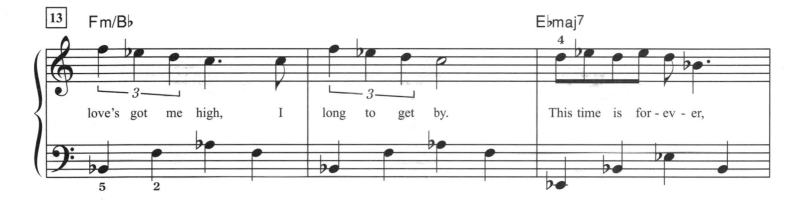

love's got me high, I long to get by. This time is for-ev-er,

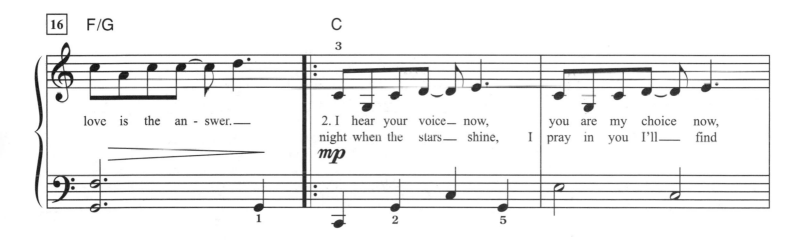

love is the an-swer. 2. I hear your voice now, you are my choice now,
night when the stars shine, I pray in you I'll find

the love you bring.
a love so true. When Heav-en's in my heart, at
morn-ing a-wakes me, will

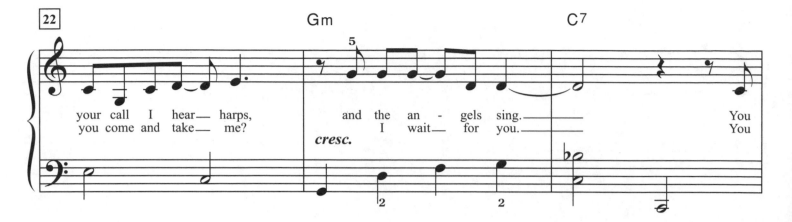

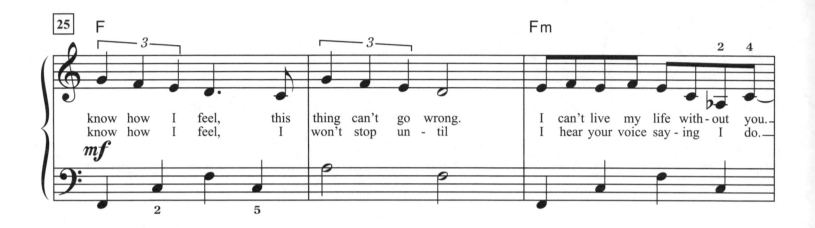

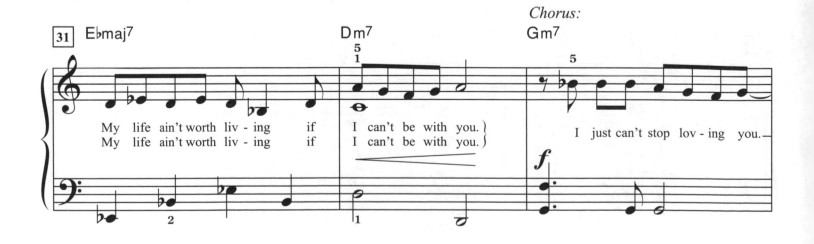

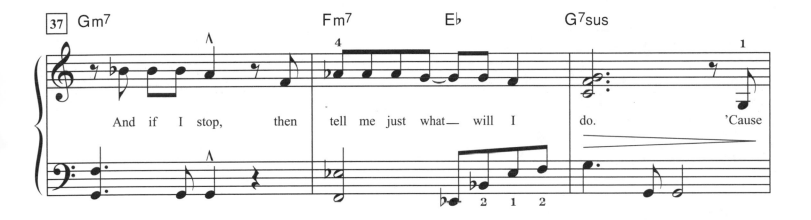

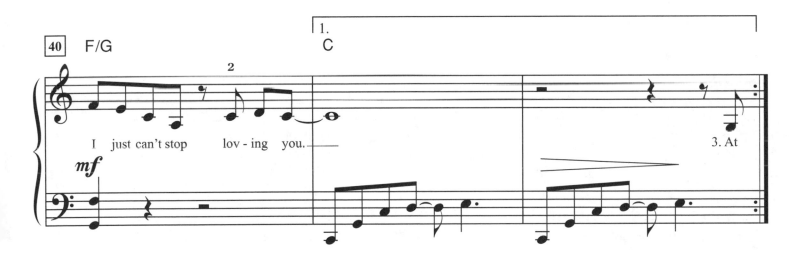

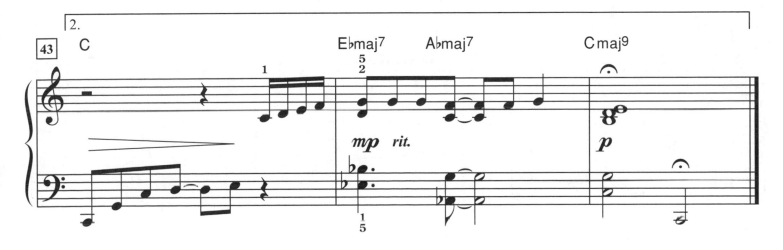

THRILLER

Words and Music by
Rod Temperton
Arranged by Dan Coates

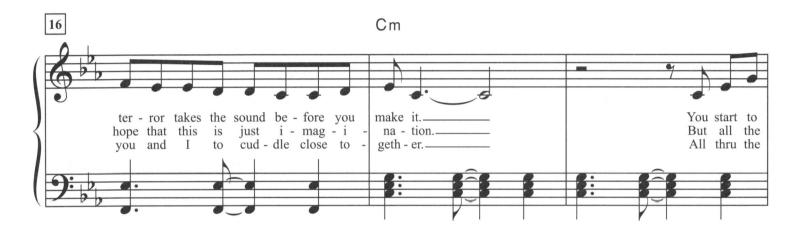

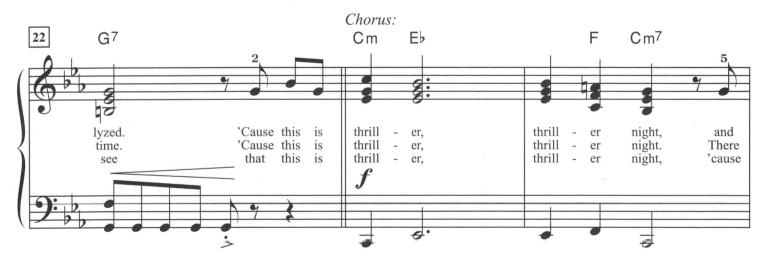

50

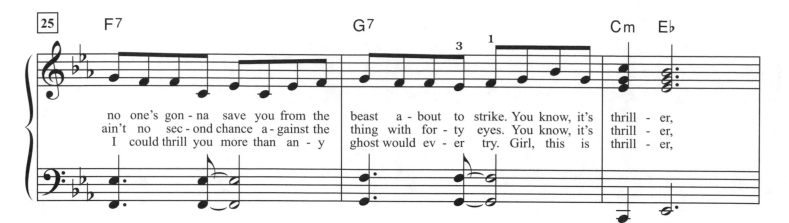

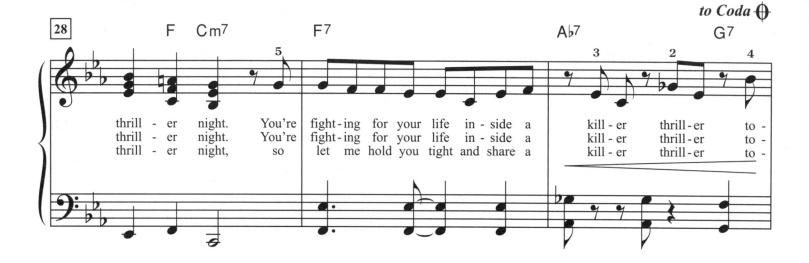

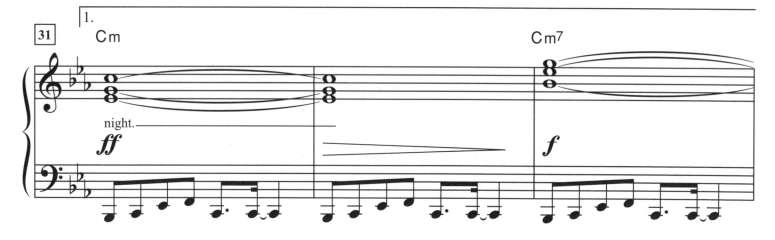

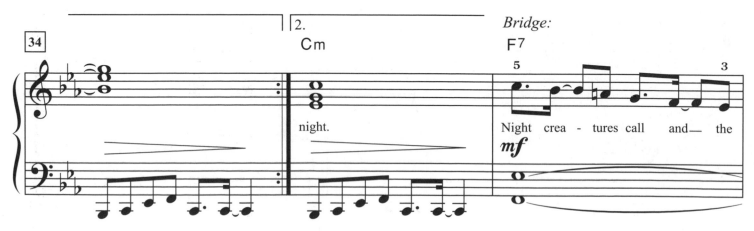

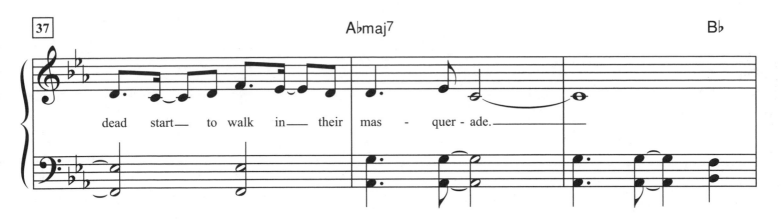

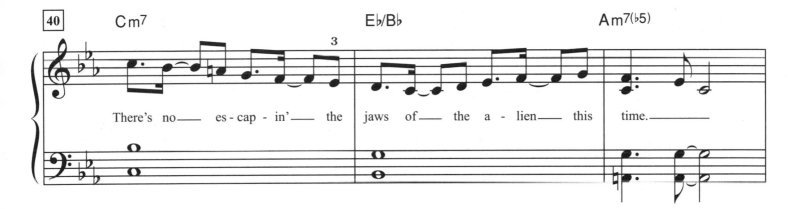

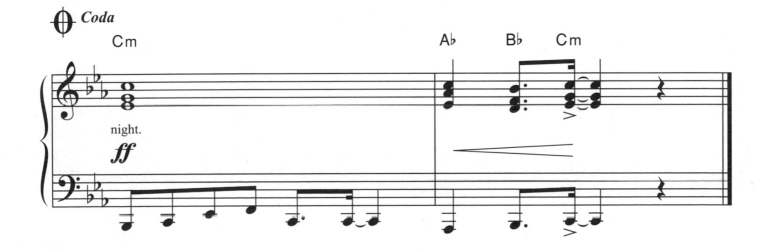

BEAT IT

Written and Composed by
Michael Jackson
Arranged by Dan Coates

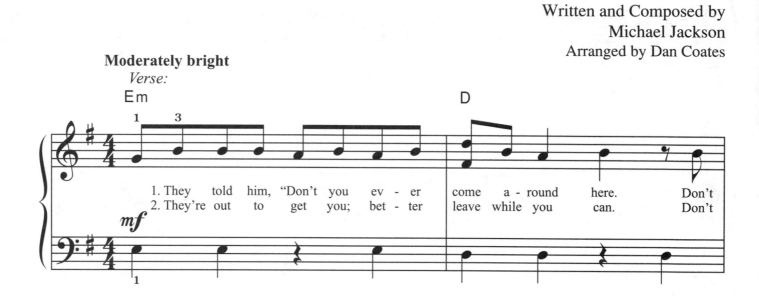

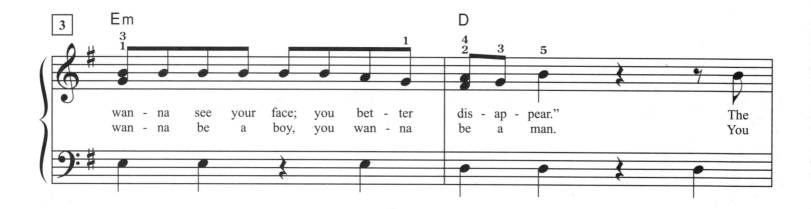

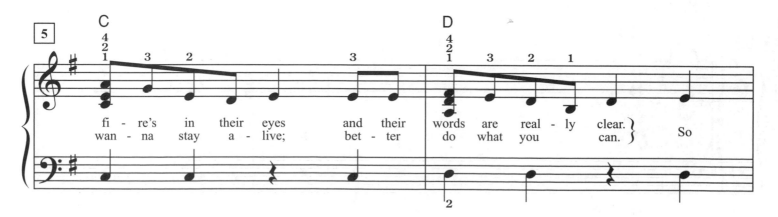

53

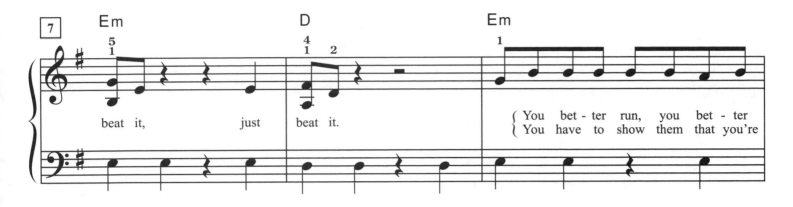

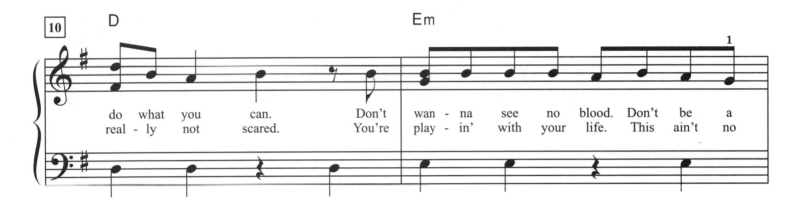

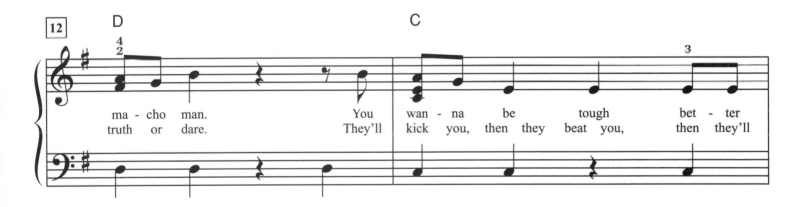

Chorus:

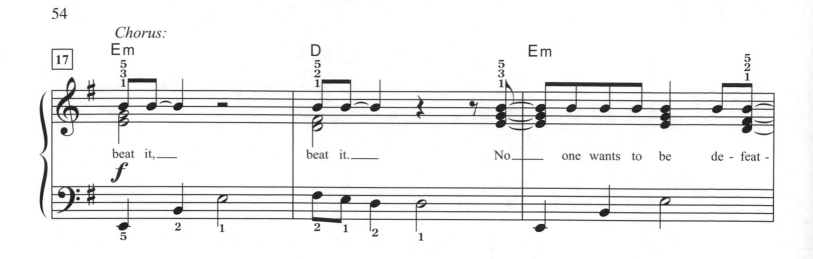

beat it,___   beat it.___   No___ one wants to be de - feat -

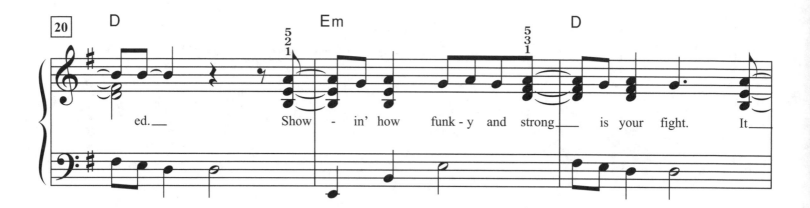

ed.___   Show - in' how   funk - y and strong___ is your fight.   It___

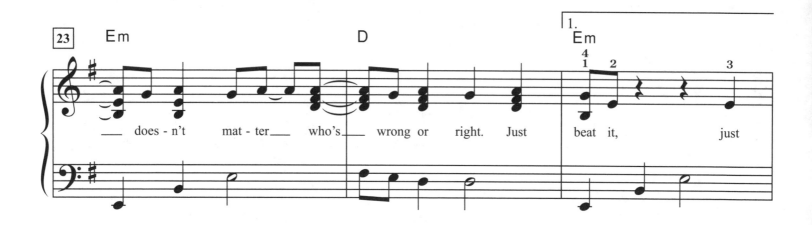

___ does - n't   mat - ter___ who's ___ wrong or   right.   Just   beat it,   just

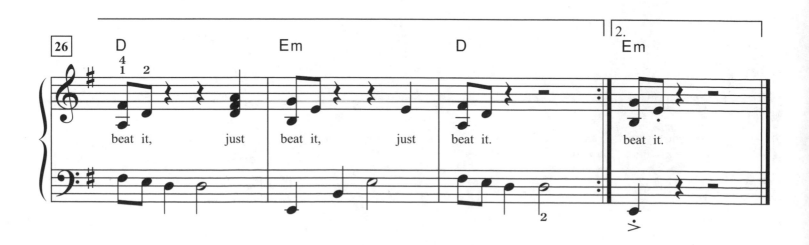

beat it,   just   beat it,   just   beat it.   beat it.

BLACK OR WHITE

Written and Composed by Michael Jackson
Rap Lyrics Written by Bill Bottrell
Arranged by Dan Coates

Bright dance beat

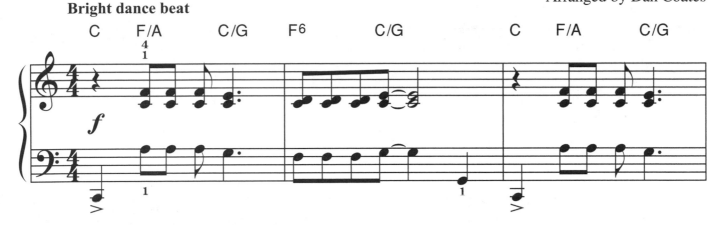

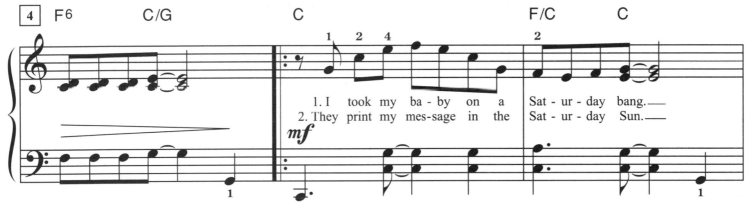

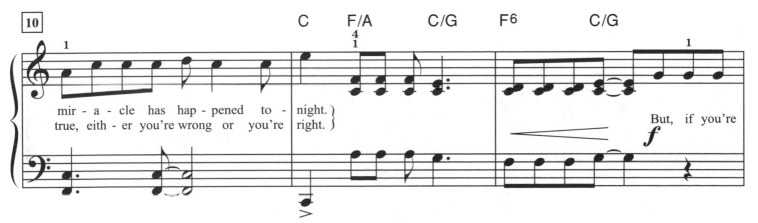

think-in' a - bout my ba - by, it don't mat - ter if you're black or white.

1. F/A C/G F6 C/G

2. F/A C/G

F6 C/G F

Now tell me you a - gree with me when I saw you kick-ing dirt in my

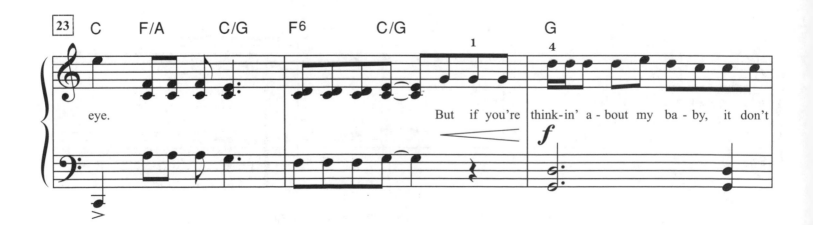

C F/A C/G F6 C/G G

eye. But if you're think-in' a - bout my ba - by, it don't

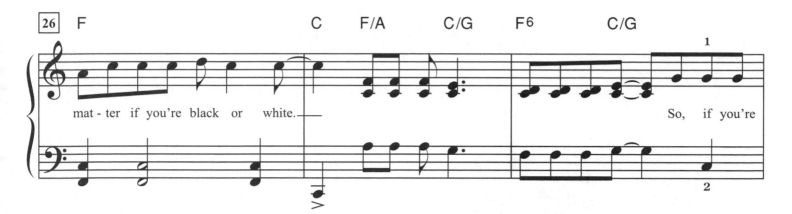

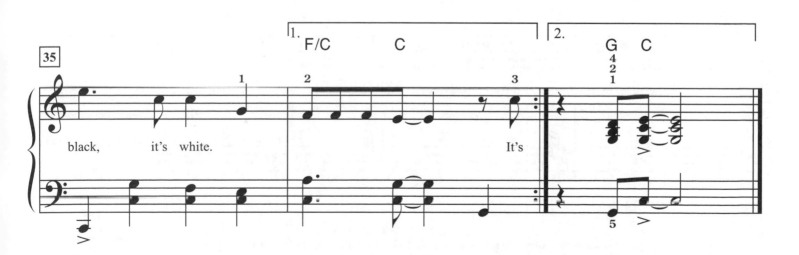

EARTH SONG

Words and Music by
Michael Jackson
Arranged by Dan Coates

Slowly

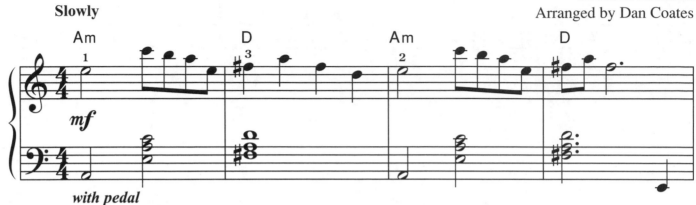

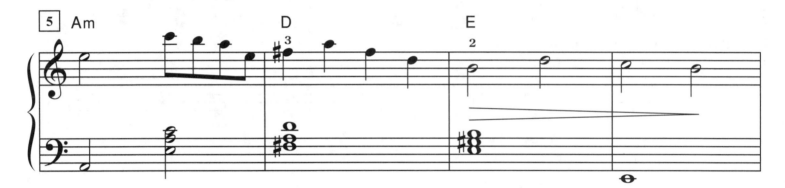

Verse:

1. What a - bout sun - rise, what a - bout rain?
2. What have we done to the world? look what we've done.

What a - bout all the things that you said we were— to gain?
What a - bout all the peace that you pledge your on - ly son?

59

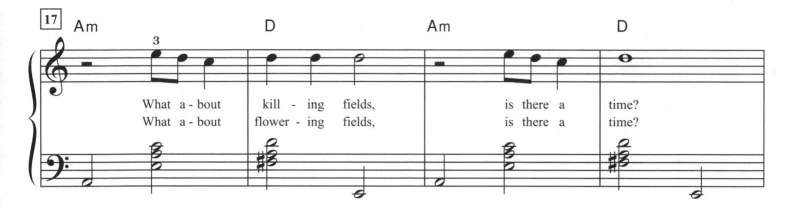

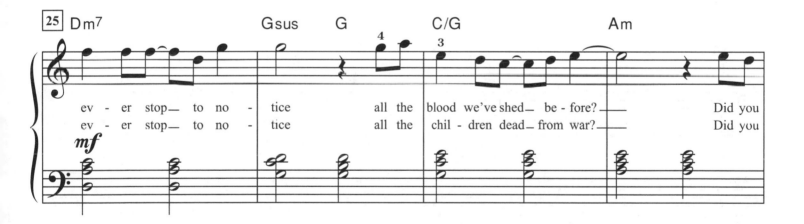

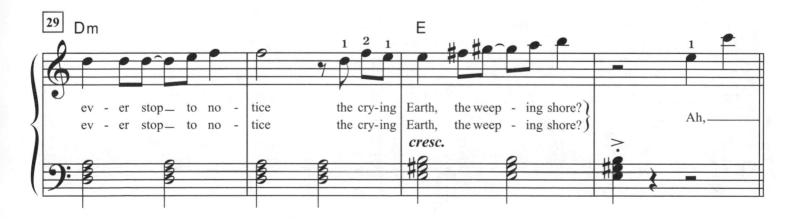

Chorus:

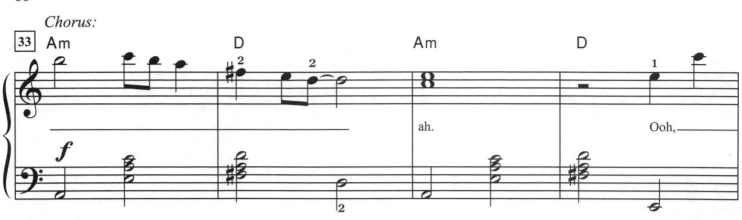

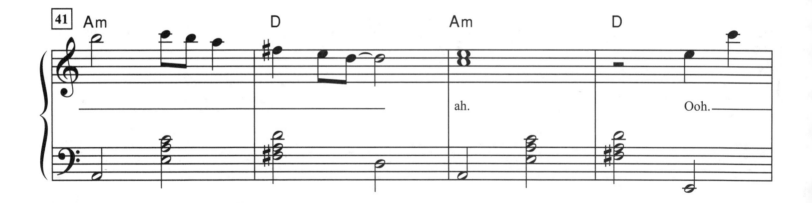

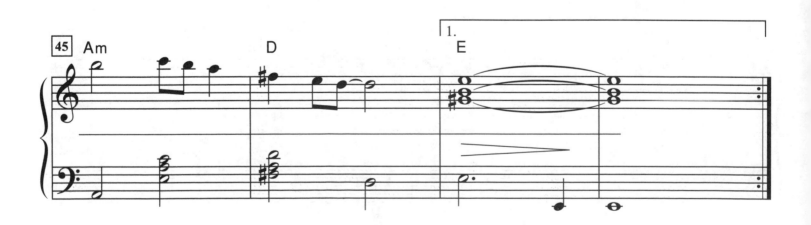

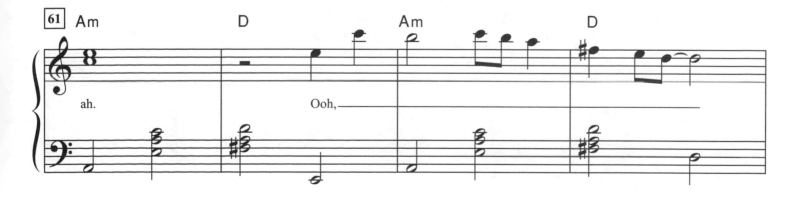

Verse:

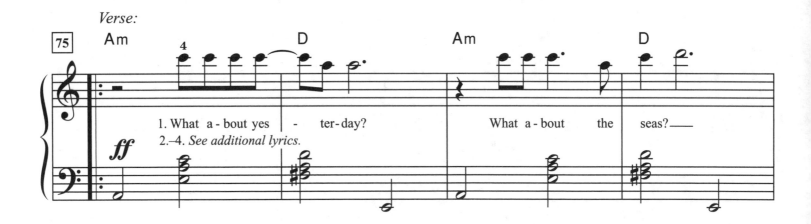

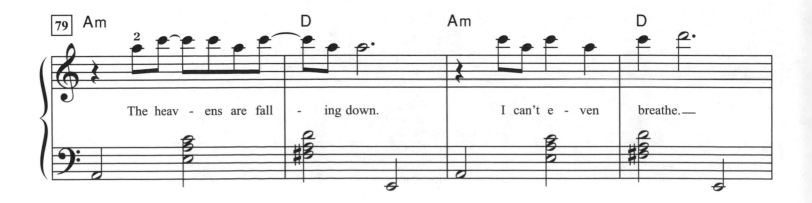

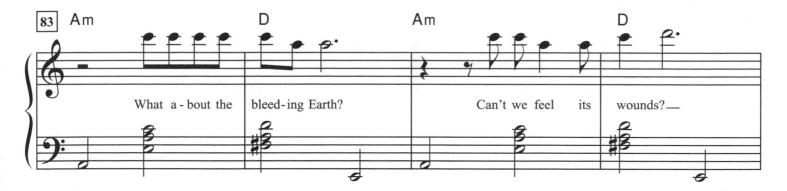

What a-bout the | bleed-ing Earth? | Can't we feel its | wounds?—

1., 2., 3., 4.

What a-bout | na-ture's worth? | It's our plan-et's | womb.—

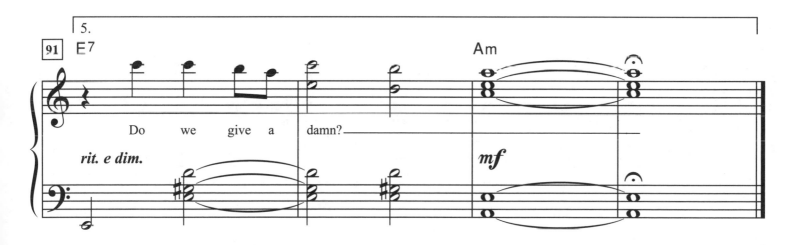

5.

rit. e dim.

Do we give a | damn?—

mf

Verse 2:
What about animals?
We've turned kingdom to dust.
What about elephants?
Have we lost their trust?
What about crying whales?
We're ravaging the seas.
What about forest trails,
Burnt despite our pleas?

Verse 3:
What about the holy land
Torn apart by creed?
What about the common man,
Can't we set him free?
What about children cying?
Can't you hear them cry?
Where did we go wrong?
Someone tell me why.

Verse 4:
What about babies?
What about the days?
What about all their joy?
What about the man?
What about the crying man?
What about Abraham?
What about death again?
Do we give a damn?

BILLIE JEAN

Written and Composed by
Michael Jackson
Arranged by Dan Coates

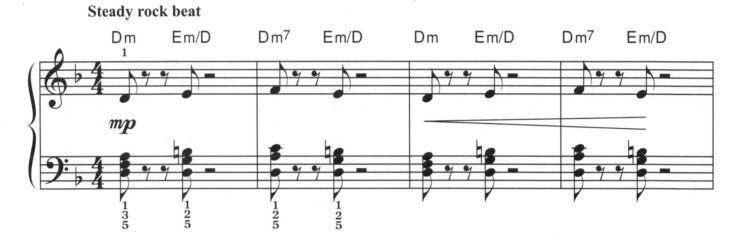

Verse:

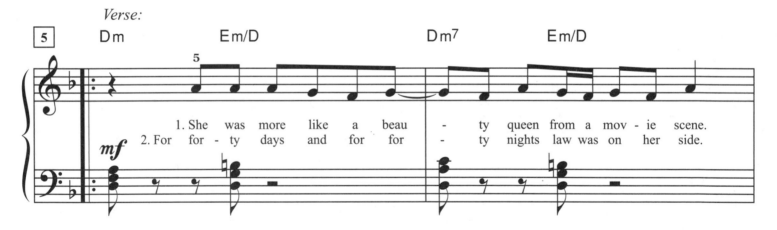

1. She was more like a beau - ty queen from a mov - ie scene.
2. For for - ty days and for for - ty nights law was on her side.

I said don't mind, but what do you mean I am the one
But who can stand when she's in de - mand, her schemes and one plans,

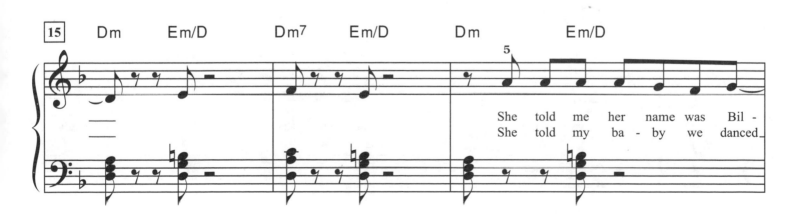

66

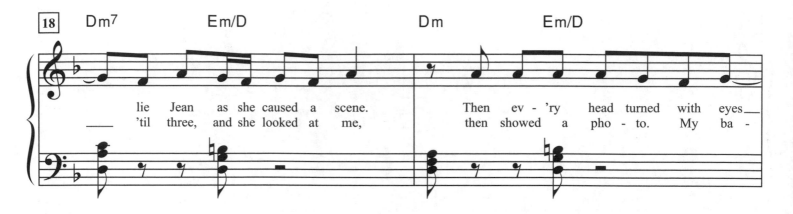

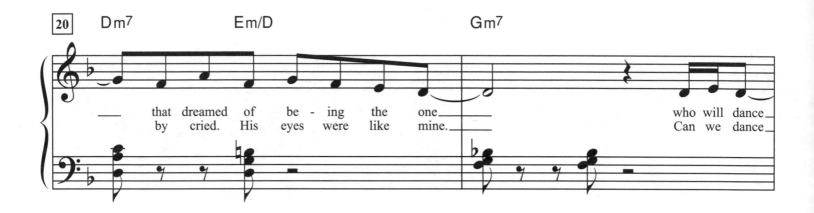

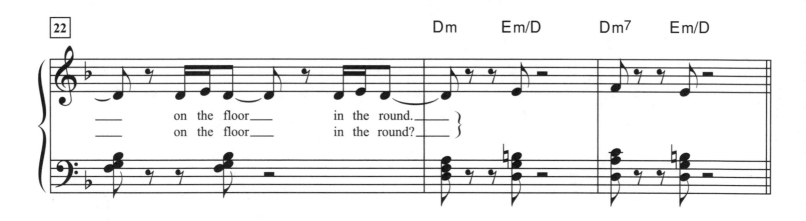

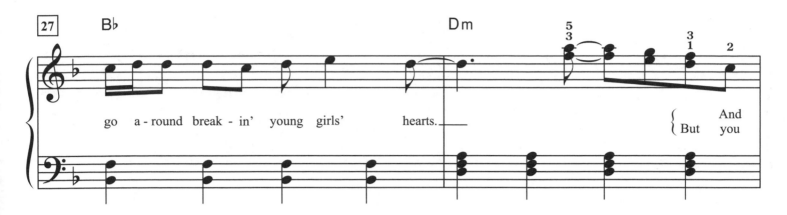

go - a-round break-in' young girls' hearts. ___ { But And you

moth - er al - ways told me be
came and stood___ right by me, just a

care - ful who___ you love, be
smell of sweet___ per - fume. This

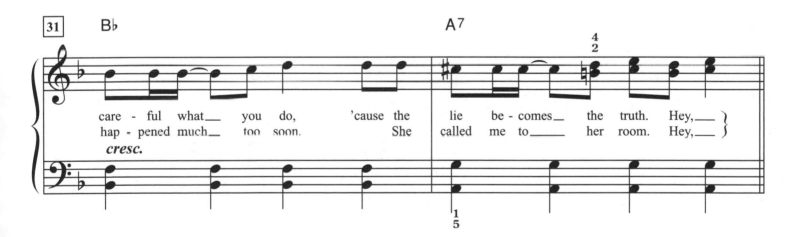

cresc.

care - ful what___ you do, 'cause the
hap - pened much___ too soon. She

lie be - comes___ the truth. Hey, ___ }
called me to___ her room. Hey, ___ }

Chorus:

f

Bil - lie Jean is not my lov - er. She's just a girl who

68

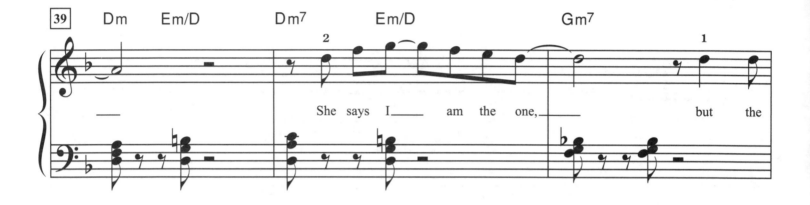

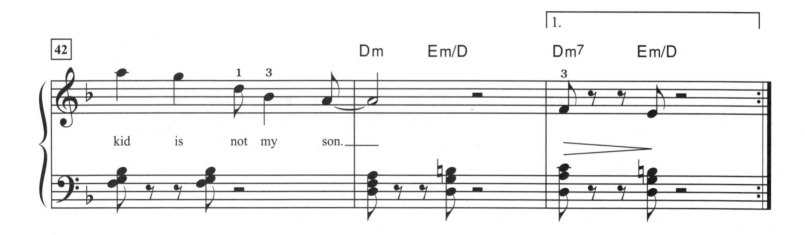

MAN IN THE MIRROR

Words and Music by
Siedah Garrett and Glen Ballard
Arranged by Dan Coates

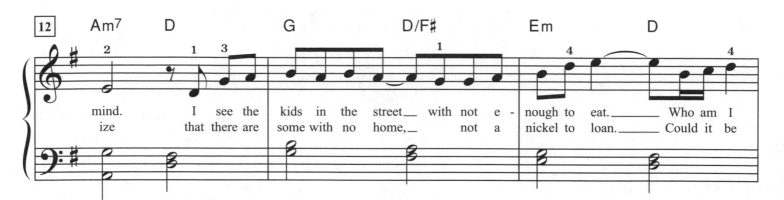

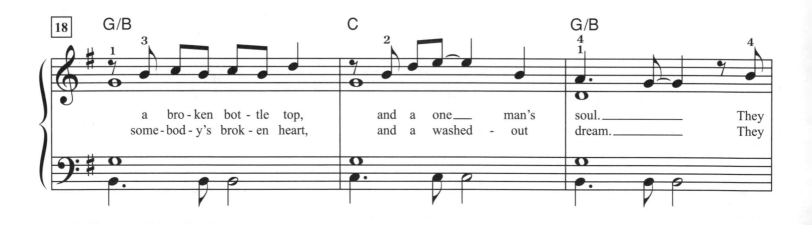

Chorus:

That's why I want you to / That's why I'm start-ing with know: } me. } I'm start-ing with the man in the mir-ror,

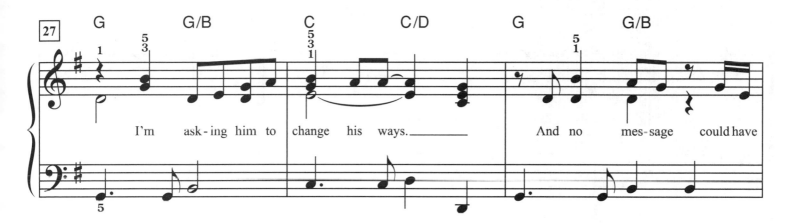

I'm ask-ing him to change his ways._____ And no mes-sage could have

been an - y clear - er: If you wan - na make the world a bet - ter place, take a

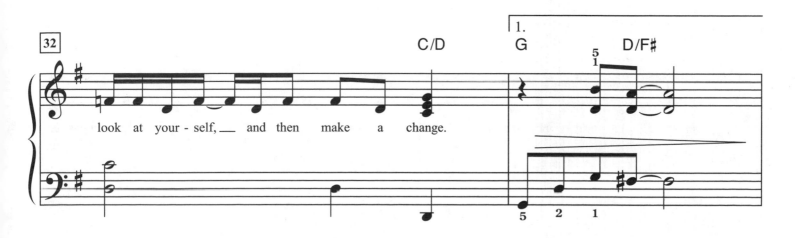

look at your - self,___ and then make a change.

get it right__ while you got the time,__ 'cause when you | close your heart__ then you close your

mind! | Na na na, na na na,___ na | na___ na na.___

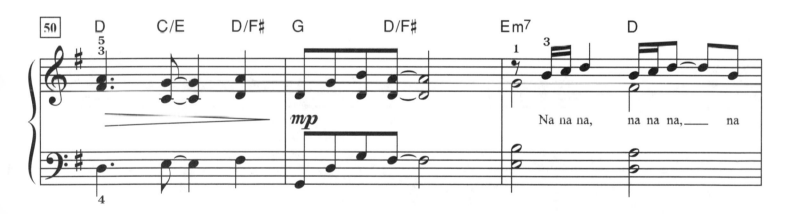

Na na na, na na na,___ na

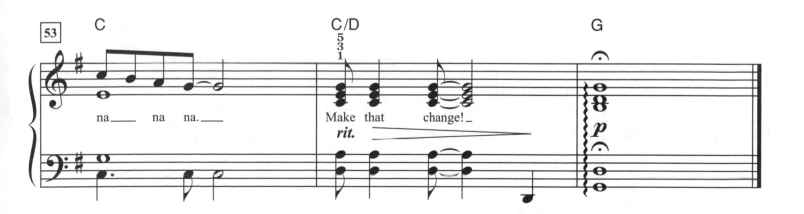

na___ na na.___ | Make that change!__ |

THIS IS IT

Written and Composed by
Michael Jackson and Paul Anka
Arranged by Dan Coates

thous - and times,   and you said_____ you real - ly know me, too, your - self.____ And I know__
thous - and years,   and you tell_____ me that you've seen my face be - fore.____ And you said__
thous - and years,   and you said_____ you want   some of this your - self.____ And you said,

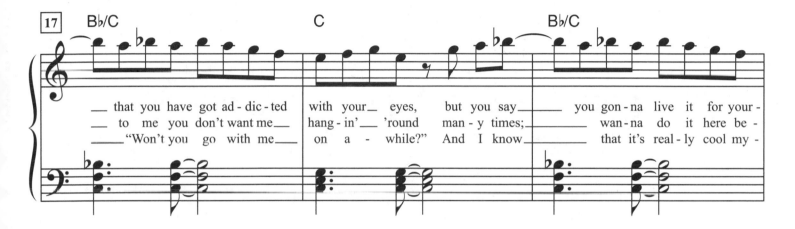

___ that you have got ad - dic - ted   with your__ eyes,   but you say____ you gon - na live it for your -
___ to me you don't want me___   hang - in' 'round   man - y times;____ wan - na do it here be -
____ "Won't you go with me___   on a - while?" And I know____ that it's real - ly cool my -

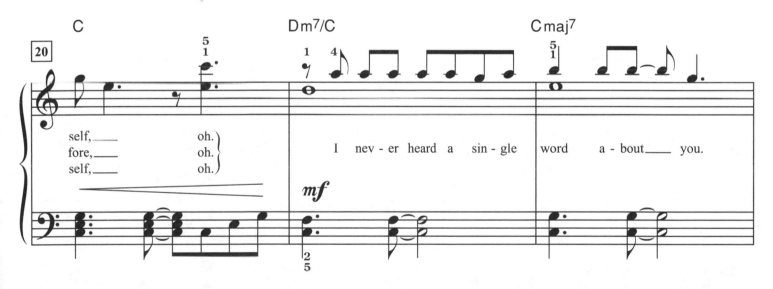

self,___   oh.)
fore,___   oh. }   I nev - er heard a sin - gle   word   a - bout___ you.
self,___   oh.)

mf

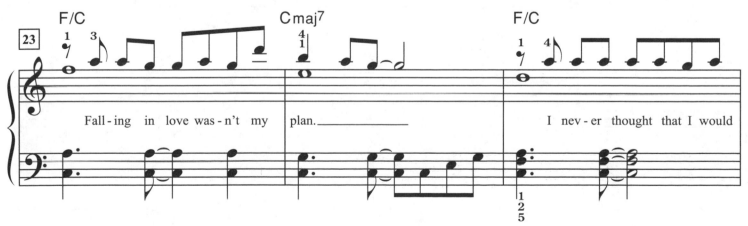

Fall - ing in love was - n't my   plan._____   I nev - er thought that I would